Seeking God's Way
Understanding the Gospel in Today's Modern World

by Mark Roberts

© 2018 One Stone Press.
All rights reserved. No part of this book may be reproduced in any form without written permission of the publisher.

Published by:
One Stone Press
979 Lovers Lane
Bowling Green, KY 42103

Printed in the United States of America

ISBN-13: 978-1-941422-37-3

www.onestone.com

Table of Contents

Welcome 5

Lesson 1: Getting to Know God 7

Lesson 2: God Communicates With You 13

Lesson 3: The Body of Christ 19

Lesson 4: God's Plan of Salvation 25

Lesson 5: Learning from the Conversions in Acts 31

Appendix A: Does God Exist? 37

Appendix B: Can the Bible Be Trusted? 41

Appendix C: Using the Bible's Chapter and Verse System 45

Appendix D: Four Reasons to Become a Christian Today 47

Discover

God's will for your life

How to be certain you are right with God

Six marks of churches that please God

Five essential steps to real Christianity

How to Use This Material

1. Study each lesson carefully. Filling in the blanks in each lesson powerfully assists the learning process. Maximize the value of this material by working the lessons before class.

2. Set aside a certain time when you will study the Bible and fill in the lesson book. If you can do this at a time when you will not be interrupted, it will be to your advantage.

3. Study in a quiet place where you will not be disturbed.

4. Review the past lesson briefly before starting the next lesson.

5. Write any questions or comments in the space in the margins.

6. Areas with a star beside them (★) represent points that should be given particular attention.

This workbook was written by Mark Roberts, a Christian who simply wants to help others come to know Jesus Christ and obey His word. Numerous individuals helped the writer prepare this material by sharing their experiences, insights, and ideas. All of these are a part of this publication, and their help is gratefully acknowledged.

Seeking God's Way is designed to be used in a teaching arrangement. If, by chance, you received this material without someone to teach it, and you have questions or need assistance, please write to the publisher's address. We will do everything possible to help you find and obey the Lord. May God bless you as you seek Him.

Welcome

Welcome to your own personalized home Bible study course. As you work through these lessons you will be seeking God's will for your life in a way that is simple to understand and easy to apply in your life and circumstances.

It is extremely important to realize that the truths contained in this booklet are not the wisdom of men, or the doctrine of men. Every point is confirmed with Bible passages, proving that it is from God. Nothing less will do when dealing with the eternally important subject of your soul's final destiny.

These lessons begin with two basic, fundamental assumptions:

First, we are assuming that you believe in God. If you do not believe in the one God of the Bible, please turn to Appendix A in the back of this book where some basic proofs for the existence of God are given.

Second, as indicated above, we accept the Bible as the verbally inspired, absolutely perfect word of God. If you believe the Bible is anything less than a perfect book from heaven, please turn to Appendix B where proofs of the Bible's inerrancy and accuracy are given.

The lessons ask you to look up various passages of scripture and answer simple questions. Because it is readily available and very reliable, we have used the New King James Version of the Bible in preparing these lessons. If you do not know how to use the Bible's chapter and verse system please see Appendix C which will explain how to find references in your Bible. If you do not have a Bible, please let those who set up this study know immediately, and they will provide you with a Bible of your own.

Study carefully, write any questions or comments you have in the margins (where additional space has been given), and enjoy learning the living word of God!

Lesson 1

Getting to Know God

The Bible begins with the impressive words, "In the beginning God" (Genesis 1:1). Who is God? How can we learn more about Him? Is it important to know God?

LESSON OBJECTIVE: Learn who the God of the Bible is.

I. **Who is God?**

  A. Defining God is an almost impossible task because of the limitations of our mortal mind. However, the Bible helps us know and understand the Lord:

  B. God is eternal, without beginning and without end: "The _____ God is your refuge, And _____ are the everlasting arms" (Deuteronomy 33:27).

  C. God is a Spirit: "God is _____, and those who worship Him must worship in _____ and _____" (John 4:24).

  D. God is omniscient, which means all knowing. Read Psalms 139:1-6 and contemplate the Lord's infinite knowledge.

  E. God is completely good and incapable of evil: "So He said to him, 'Why do you call Me good? _____ one is _____ but _____, that is, _____.'" (Matthew 19:17).

  F. God is complete love: "He who does not love does not know God, for _____ is _____" (1 John 4:8).

  G. God is totally just toward all wrongdoing: "Beloved, do not avenge yourselves, but rather give place to wrath; for it is written, '_____ is Mine, I will _____,' says the _____" (Romans 12:19).

   1. "For our God is a _____ fire" (Hebrews 12:29).

   2. Do you understand that God's love and justice are not contradictory (see Jeremiah 9:24)? _____

H. God is the Creator of everything: "For in six days the _____ made the heavens and the _____, the sea, and _____ that is in them, and _____ the seventh day" (Exodus 20:11).

I. Summary: God is the eternal Creator, who knows all and exercises love, mercy and justice toward all. These are the facts about God. We come to know God by focusing on four key characteristics of God.

II. God is dependable.

A. God is not changeable: "the Father of lights, with whom there is no _____ or shadow of _____" (James 1:17).

B. God is not a liar: "God, _____ cannot _____" (Titus 1:2).

C. God is not mistaken or ever in error: "As for God, His _____ is _____." (Psalm 18:30).

D. You can count on God! He will not vary, lie, or make a mistake.

III. God is powerful.

God's limitless power is seen in a number of ways in the Scriptures. Consider:

A. He created everything. Genesis 1:1-31 records the beginning of all life, spoken into existence by the Lord.

B. He rules the universe: "till you know that the Most High _____ in the _____ of men, and gives it to whomever _____ chooses" (Daniel 4:25).

C. He has the power of life and death: "And the Lord God formed man of the dust of the ground, and breathed into his nostrils the _____ of _____ and man became a living being" (Genesis 2:7).

D. He knows the future and can foretell it: "God, who gives _____ to the dead and calls those things which do not _____ as though they _____" (Romans 4:17).

E. Such a Being as this is obviously worthy of our attention, and our praise!

LESSON 1 Getting to Know God

IV. God is unique.

A. There is only one God: "The Lord our God, the Lord is _____" (Deuteronomy 6:4).

B. No other beings are equal to or higher than God: "Now see that I, even I, am He, And there is _____ God _____ Me" (Deuteronomy 32:39).

C. No other being is like God: "Remember the former things of old: for I am God, and there is _____ other; I am God, and there is _____ like _____" (Isaiah 46:9).

D. No other being loves mankind like God does: "For God so _____ the world that He _____ His only begotten Son, that whoever believes in Him should not perish but have everlasting life" (John 3:16).

V. God has complete authority.

A. Authority is the right to command and expect obedience. God possesses complete and absolute authority. He has the undisputed right to command all people. Why?

B. He created us: "So God _____ man in His own image, in the image of God He created him; male and female He _____ them" (Genesis 1:27).

   1. Humans are not God. We cannot tell the Lord what to do.

   2. "O man, _____ are you to reply against God? Will the _____ formed say to him who formed it, 'Why have you _____ me like this?'" (Romans 9:20).

C. He rules the universe. Read Psalm 2. It is apparent that the kings of this earth have no power when compared to the Lord's awesome strength.

D. He will judge us: "Because He has appointed a _____ on which He will judge the _____ in righteousness by the Man whom He has _____. He has given _____ of this to all by raising Him from the _____" (Acts 17:31).

10 Seeking God's Way

    E. He knows what is best for us: "and to keep the _____ of the Lord and His statutes which I _____ you today for your _____?" (Deuteronomy 10:13). We will learn of His good commands in the next lesson.

VI. How does man stand before God?

    A. As people come to know how great and wonderful God is, they want to know what God thinks of them. Does He know me? What does He think of me?

    B. God knows and loves all people (John 3:16).

    C. He wants everyone to come and live with Him in heaven for all eternity (2 Peter 3:9; 1 Timothy 2:3-4).

    D. However, sin destroys our relationship with God and our hope of going to heaven when we die.

        1. Sin is the violation of God's law (1 John 3:4). Sin separates us from God. Why? Because a perfect, just, and holy God cannot overlook sin, or pretend that sin is not significant. Sin matters to God!

        2. "But your _____ have _____ you from your _____; And your sins have _____ His face from you, So that _____ will not _____" (Isaiah 59:2).

        3. "For the _____ of _____ is death" (Romans 6:23).

★   E. God loves you so much that He does not want you to die in your sins and be eternally separated from Him. Without God we would have no hope, but He has a plan to fix our sin problem.

    F. Remember, we are the ones who have wronged God by violating His law. Thus, we must do as He says. As sinners, we cannot dictate the terms of forgiveness!

    G. God's plan to rescue us from our sins may be different from what men would propose, but God's ways are not man's ways: "'For My _____ are not your _____, Nor are your ways My ways,'" says the Lord. For as the _____ are higher than the _____, So are My ways _____ than your _____, And My _____ than your thoughts" (Isaiah 55:8-9).

H. Obedience to God is the key factor in our relationship with Him. God will save us from our sins only if we completely submit to His authority and His plan (1 Peter 5:6).

VII. Conclusion

A. God is the eternal, all-knowing, all-powerful Being that loves us more than anyone else. He is a unique, dependable God that you can trust with your soul's eternal destiny. This is the God of the Bible—not a man-made deity.

B. God wants you to be in His family and to come live with Him for all time in heaven.

C. Sin blocks man from being in a relationship with God and going to heaven.

D. God loves us too much to let us remain in our sins, and so He has mounted a rescue operation to save sinful people. This plan will only work for those who completely submit themselves to God's will and authority. Are you interested in learning about this plan? _____

E. Lesson 2 will show you where this plan is found, and how you can know that it is God's plan.

What is the Bible all about?
From beginning to end, it is the record of God's plan to save humanity from sin.

Lesson 2

God Communicates With You

In the last lesson we learned who God is and that we must obey Him. But, God is in heaven, and we are on earth. How can we learn what God wants us to do?

LESSON OBJECTIVE: Understand the New Testament as our sole guide in all matters of faith and practice.

I. **Jesus is God's way of communicating with you.**
   God has used many different ways of speaking to people in times past, but now...

   A. He speaks to us through His Son: "God, who at various _____ and in different _____ spoke in time past to the fathers by the _____, has in these last days spoken to us by His _____, whom He has _____ heir of all things, through whom also He _____ the worlds" (Hebrews 1:1-2).

   B. Jesus is fully vested with the complete authority of God: "Jesus came and spoke to them, saying, 'All _____ has been given to Me in _____ and on _____'" (Matthew 28:18).

   C. Jesus leads us to the Father: "Jesus said to him, '____ am the _____, the _____, and the _____. No one comes to the _____ except through Me'" (John 14:6).

   D. Obeying Jesus is the same as obeying God, because Jesus is deity (John 1:1, 14).

II. **Jesus speaks to us by His authorized apostles.**

   A. Christ has returned to heaven (Acts 1:9). He no longer speaks directly to people but revealed His will to specially chosen messengers, the apostles.

   B. "So Jesus said to them again, 'Peace to you! As the _____ has sent _____, I also _____ you'" (John 20:21).

C. The apostles have tremendous credibility as witnesses of Christ because they were heavily persecuted (and even killed) for teaching about Jesus. Who would suffer or die for a lie?

D. When we obey the teaching of the apostles, it is the same as obeying Jesus (see 1 Corinthians 14:37).

III. How does God speak to us today?

A. The apostles have all died. They cannot personally tell us what Jesus said.

B. Further, there can be no more apostles today. Note the qualifications to be an apostle, which are given in Acts 1:21-22:

1. An apostle must have been personally with _____ (v. 21) from the time of John's _____ until the ascension of Christ (v. 22).

2. Can anyone meet these requirements today? _____

C. However, before the apostles died God directed them to write down the commands and teachings of Jesus (see 2 Peter 1:20-22; 1 Corinthians 4:6). We call this the New Testament.

1. The Holy Spirit guided these writings: "The Helper, the _____ _____, whom the _____ will send in My name, _____ will _____ you all things, and bring to your remembrance all things that I said to you" (John 14:26).

2. "However, when He, the _____ of _____, has come, _____ will guide you into all _____; for He will not speak on His own _____, but whatever He hears He will speak" (John 16:13).

D. Reading the apostles' writings enables us to obey God: "By which, when you read, you may _____ my knowledge in the mystery of Christ, which in other ages was _____ made _____ to the sons of men, as it has _____ been _____ by the Spirit to His holy apostles and prophets" (Ephesians 3:4-5).

LESSON 2 God Communicates With You 15

The New Testament is a blueprint that equips us completely to obey God (2 Timothy 1:13; 3:16-17). God speaks to you today through the New Testament.

E. Obeying what the New Testament teaches is how we obey God today, because the New Testament is God's word.

IV. **How must we treat God's word, the New Testament?**

A. Careless handling of God's commands results in serious consequences. The Lord expects people to do exactly as He instructs.

B. Read the story of Adam and Eve (Genesis 3:1-10). What did they do that was wrong? _____ Had God told them not to do this (Genesis 2:16-17)? _____ What was the result of their sin? _____

C. Read the story of Uzzah (2 Samuel 6:3-7). What did he do? _____ Was this forbidden (Numbers 4:15)? _____ How was Uzzah punished?_____

D. It is our obligation to handle the word of God rightly: "Be _____ to present yourself _____ to God, a worker who does not need to be ashamed, rightly _____ the word of truth" (2 Timothy 2:15).

E. It is obvious that God's word is not to be ignored or halfway obeyed. We must do what God says!

F. Therefore, nothing can be substituted for His commands: "But even if we, or an angel from heaven, preach _____ other _____ to you than what we have preached to you, let him be _____" (Galatians 1:8-9).

G. The New Testament is God's complete and final revelation to man.

1. "...exhorting you to _____ earnestly for the faith which was _____ for all _____ to the saints" (Jude 1:3).

2. Read Acts 6:7. What is "the faith"? _____

H. This means that the New Testament is an "exclusive contract." Nothing else contains the word of God, or is vested with His authority.

V. False standards of right and wrong.

A. Unfortunately, not everyone is willing to obey just the New Testament. Let's examine some false standards of right and wrong.

B. "I'll do what the majority of people do...the majority is right."

1. Read Matthew 7:13-14 and see if the majority of people actually is right. What does the Bible say? _____
   _____

2. Jesus tells us how many can be expected to enter heaven in Luke 13:23-24. What does He say? _____
   _____

C. "My conscience is my guide." The conscience is our inner sense of what is right and wrong. It is that "little voice" that causes guilt when we violate our own personal standards of morality. The conscience can help in keeping us from doing wrong but is not perfect because sin can destroy it:

1. "Speaking lies...having their own _____ seared with a hot iron" (1 Timothy 4:2).

2. Paul persecuted the church before he became a Christian, but he said "I have lived in all _____ conscience before _____ until this day" (Acts 23:1).

D. "I trust my preacher or creed books or parents." Many people depend on theologians, pastors, preachers, books, or what mother and father say.

1. According to 1 Corinthians 2:5 should we place our faith in men? _____

2. "He who loves _____ or _____ more than Me is not _____ of Me. And he who loves _____ or _____ more than Me is not worthy of Me" (Matthew 10:37).

E. "I feel that I am right." Are feelings really an infallible guide to judging our relationship with God?

1. Read Proverbs 14:12. Can we trust our feelings? _____

2. What does Jeremiah 10:23 say about this? _____
_____

F. "I follow the Ten Commandments and Law of Moses." We are no longer under Moses' Law which was for the Jews only. "Therefore the law was our _____ to bring us to Christ, that we might be justified by faith. But after faith has come, we are _____ longer _____ a tutor" (Galatians 3:24-25).

VI. Conclusion

A. We must obey God to be forgiven of our sins. The only way that we can know what God wants us to do (so that we can obey Him) is through the New Testament that His Son revealed to the apostles. We must accept the New Testament as our only guide in all matters of faith and practice.

B. Are you ready to let the New Testament be your only guide? _____

C. There are so many different churches today. How is one to know which church is correct? By using our exclusive guide, the New Testament, which was given to us by God, we can find the church that is part of His plan to save us from sin. This will be our goal in Lesson 3.

> There is a **way** that seems **right** to a man, but its **end** is the way of **death**.
> - Proverbs 14:12

18 Seeking God's Way

Lesson 3

The Body of Christ

Religion in America is a confused mess of conflicting doctrines and churches. To sort through it all we must use the New Testament, to direct us to the church Jesus built.

LESSON OBJECTIVE: To find the true church that pleases God.

I. **Why is it important to find the right church?**

   A. Because the right church, Christ's church, has tremendous value. Jesus bought the church personally. Read Acts 20:28 and 1 Peter 1:18-19. What did Jesus purchase the church with? _____

   B. Because Christ's church is in God's eternal plan: "To the intent that now the manifold _____ of God might be made known by the _____ to the principalities and powers in the _____ places, according to the _____ purpose which He accomplished in _____ _____ our Lord" (Ephesians 3:10-11).

   C. Because Christ's church practices pure New Testament Christianity. Churches that do not completely follow Christ's will, as revealed in the New Testament, inevitably teach and preach false doctrine and error. Joining with such a group is not pleasing to Jesus (2 John 9; Galatians 1:8-9).

II. **How many churches are there?**

   A. The New Testament tells us there is only one church:

      1. "And He is the _____ of the body, the _____" (Colossians 1:18).

      2. "There is one _____ and one _____, just as you were called in one _____ of your calling" (Ephesians 4:4).

   B. If the church is the body (Colossians 1:18) and there is only one body (Ephesians 4:4), how many churches are there? _____

C. Denominational division is sinful and wrong: "Now I plead with you, brethren, by the name of our Lord _____ _____, that you all speak the _____ thing, and that there be no _____ among you, but that you be perfectly joined together in the _____ mind and in the _____ judgment" (1 Corinthians 1:10).

D. Jesus only built one church: His church (Matthew 16:18). Jesus actually prayed for unity, not denominational division: "That they all may be _____, as You, Father, are in Me, and I in You; that they also may be _____ in Us, that the world may _____ that You sent _____" (John 17:21).

III. The church is not:

A. A material building. "God, who made the world and everything in it, since He is Lord of heaven and earth, does _____ dwell in _____ made with _____" (Acts 17:24). Instead, the church is a spiritual relationship.

B. A social club. The church is a spiritual institution, not a place for parties and fun. Read Romans 14:17. Is the church designed for spiritual work and righteousness or recreation and social activity?
_____

C. A denomination. A denomination is a coalition of many congregations who are under one governing body. That governing body determines what every church in the group must practice and believe.

1. Such a plan does not come from God. The Bible says nothing about any denominational hierarchy, organization, creed or name.

2. Instead, the New Testament teaches undenominational Christianity. This means each congregation is autonomous and independent of all other churches (see Acts 14:23; 1 Peter 5:2; Titus 1:5).

3. No group of humans determines what Jesus' church does. The Lord's church rejects all human creeds so that it can follow the head of the church, Jesus (see Ephesians 1:22-23; Galatians 1:8-9).

LESSON 3 The Body of Christ 21

D. An institution that dispenses salvation. Some think being saved is merely a matter of having one's name on the "right" church's roll. This is incorrect.

1. Read Ephesians 5:23. Who saves, Jesus or an institution?
   _____

2. The Lord's church is simply people who belong to Christ. When people were saved they were _____ to the number of others who were also saved (Acts 2:47).

3. Thus, the church is a relationship with Jesus and other Christians, not a club or association that has the power of salvation in itself.

IV. **How can we find the church that pleases God?**
By reading the New Testament, we can learn what God wants His church to do and be. Then we can be part of a group practicing genuine New Testament Christianity.

A. The name the church wears: The church that belongs to Christ should wear a name given in the New Testament, instead of a name of human origin.

1. Romans 16:16 gives a name for the Lord's people: "The churches of _____ greet you." The New Testament lists two other similar names for the church (see Acts 20:28 and Hebrews 12:23). All of these terms identify one group: the Lord's church, the church of Christ.

2. What name do members of Christ's church wear (see Acts 11:26)? _____

B. The work the church should do: God has commissioned the church, through the New Testament, to do only three activities.

1. Preach the gospel (see 1 Thessalonians 1:8).

2. Help needy Christians (see 2 Corinthians 8; 1 Timothy 5:16).

3. Teach Christians so that they will be spiritually stronger (see Acts 20:32).

★ The church must not dilute its function and efforts by taking on additional duties that God does not desire for it to do.

C. The guide the church must use
   1. There is only one way to be certain we are pleasing God: follow His Word, the New Testament. "And whatever you do in word or deed, do _____ in the _____ of the Lord _____" (Colossians 3:17).
   2. When a policeman says, "Stop in the name of the law," he means "I'm ordering you to stop by the authority of the law." When Paul says, "Act only in the name of Jesus" he means we should act only by the authority of _____.
   3. How is Jesus' authority expressed to us today? _____
   _____

D. The organization of the church
   1. Jesus is the head of His church: "and gave Him to be _____ over all things to the _____, which is His _____" (Ephesians 1:22-23).
   2. The only "offices" the New Testament church has are elders (also called bishops or pastors) and deacons (Philippians 1:1).

E. The worship of the church
   1. "God is Spirit, and those who worship _____ must worship in _____ and _____" (John 4:24).
   2. Worship that pleases us, but not God, is absolutely worthless. Read Genesis 4:3-8. Was the Lord pleased with Cain's worship? _____
   3. Read Matthew 15:9. What makes worship vain? _____
   _____
   4. Christ's church will do as He directs in every area, but especially in how it worships. The New Testament church worshipped in five basic ways:
      a. Preaching and teaching: Acts 20:7
      b. The Lord's Supper: read 1 Corinthians 11:24-26. Does just one person partake of the Lord's Supper or should everyone partake? _____

       c. Prayer: Acts 2:42

       d. Giving: 1 Corinthians 16:1-2

       e. Singing: Ephesians 5:19; Colossians 3:16

    5. Can we change God's plan for the church and still be pleasing unto the Lord? _____

  F. The teaching of the church; the Lord's plan of salvation: The church that Jesus built will teach the Lord's plan of salvation, not a plan of human devising. In our next lesson we will learn the New Testament plan of salvation.

V. Conclusion

  A. Because the church is composed of those who are in a right relationship with God, it is very important that you be part of the Lord's church.

  B. By seeing what the New Testament church did, we can find the New Testament church today. If you could find a church that is obeying the Bible and the Bible only, would you want to be a part of it? _____

  C. Since all saved people are in the Lord's church (Ephesians 5:23), the next logical question is, "How can I be saved?" We will study this question in Lesson 4.

Lesson 4

God's Plan of Salvation

People hear conflicting and differing plans of salvation every day. To escape this confusion we must find out what God says in His word, the New Testament. It and it alone will give us the truth that leads us to heaven.

LESSON OBJECTIVE: Learn how to be saved from sin.

I. **God's part: providing grace**

   A. Definition: grace is undeserved favor and is the power that saves us. "For by grace you have been saved through faith, and that not of yourselves; it is the gift of God" (Ephesians 2:8).

   B. By His grace God does what is necessary and needed for us to be saved. It is very important that you realize that God has done what we could not do ourselves:

   1. God sent His Son. "For God so _____ the world that He gave His only begotten _____, that whoever _____ in Him should not perish but have _____ life" (John 3:16).

   2. Jesus died for us. "In Him we have _____ through His _____, the forgiveness of sins" (Ephesians 1:7).

   3. The Holy Spirit revealed God's plan to man. "For prophecy never _____ by the will of _____, but holy men of God _____ as they were moved by the _____ _____" (2 Peter 1:21).

   C. It is easy to see that without God's grace we could not be saved. Grace is also essential due to our own sin.

   1. "For _____ have sinned, and fall _____ of the glory of God" (Romans 3:23).

   2. Sin is a violation of God's law (1 John 3:4) or a failure to do what is right (James 4:17).

3. Once people sin they are separated from God and therefore completely helpless and unable to save themselves.

   "But your iniquities have _____ you from your God" (Isaiah 59:2).

   "And you, who once were _____ and _____ in your mind by wicked works, yet now He has reconciled" (Colossians 1:21).

4. Furthermore, we do not want to pay the penalty or price for our wrong doings: "For the wages of sin is _____" (Romans 6:23).

D. Our sin makes it impossible for us to save ourselves. We must turn to God.

II. The human part: accepting God's great gift of salvation

A. We cannot earn salvation because it is a priceless gift.

B. However, we need to demonstrate our desire to be saved and our complete faith in God by obeying His word. What does God ask us to do?

C. Hear the Gospel: "So then _____ comes by _____, and hearing by the _____ of God" (Romans 10:17).

D. Believe the gospel's message: "But without _____ it is impossible to please Him, for he who comes to _____ must believe that He is, and that He is a rewarder of those who diligently seek Him" (Hebrews 11:6).

   1. Genuine, biblical faith is tremendously powerful. Faith is what moves a person to do all that God has commanded and be saved (see James 2:18).

   2. Deciding whether we will believe or disbelieve the message of the Gospel will determine our eternal destiny (John 8:24).

   3. As important as faith is, by itself it will not save. Read James 2:24. Will faith alone save you? _____

E. Repent of past sins.

1. God is saving us from our sinful conduct. Therefore we should turn away from that kind of living: "Then Peter said to them, '_____, and let every one of you be _____ in the name of _____ Christ for the _____ of sins'" (Acts 2:38).
2. Repentance is neither prayer nor living perfectly. But instead it is the sincere desire to no longer be involved in sin. Repentance is the fervent desire to turn away from the sinful deeds of the past and live righteously.
3. "But _____ you _____ you will all likewise _____" (Luke 13:5).

F. Confess faith in Christ.
   1. "If you _____ with your mouth the Lord Jesus and believe in your heart that God has raised Him from the dead, you will be _____" (Romans 10:9).
   2. We must not be ashamed of Jesus but be willing to openly proclaim that we believe He is the Savior of the world.

G. Be baptized: "which now _____ us, baptism" (1 Peter 3:21).
   1. Baptism is not an outward symbol that we have already been saved. Read Acts 2:38 and Acts 22:16. What does baptism do (what is its purpose)? _____
   _____
   2. It is also important that we use the right mode of baptism. Read Romans 6:3-4. Baptism is a burial. Circle the method that is most like a burial:
      a. Sprinkling a little water on someone
      b. Pouring water on a person
      c. Being completely immersed in water

H. Is baptism really essential and necessary to be saved?
   1. Baptism places one in Christ: "For as many of you as were baptized into Christ have put on Christ" (Galatians 3:27).
   2. Who would want to be outside of Christ? _____
   Who can be saved outside of Christ? _____

3. The New Testament is clear: baptism, and nothing else, will give one entry into Christ.

4. Read Mark 16:16. There are two classes of people in this verse: those who believe in Jesus and those who do not. Jesus says that all believers will do what? They will be _____.

I. Be faithful unto death: "Be _____ until _____, and I will give you the _____ of life" (Revelation 2:10).

1. When Christians sin (and they do) they must repent, confess that sin and pray for forgiveness. "If we _____ our sins, He is faithful and just to _____ us our _____ and to _____ us from all unrighteousness" (1 John 1:9).

2. Faithfulness includes worshipping God (Hebrews 10:25), Bible study (2 Timothy 3:16), prayer (1 Thessalonians 5:17), and growing spiritually (2 Peter 1:5-8).

3. The key to faithfulness is to be more like Jesus every day: "For to this you were called, because _____ also suffered for us, leaving us an _____, that you should follow His steps" (1 Peter 2:21).

III. Summary of all we have learned

A. God is the great, all-knowing, powerful Being who loves you.

B. Your sins separate you from God.

C. God makes it possible for all to be saved; you only have to obey His plan in faith.

D. That plan is communicated to you through the New Testament.

E. Check each part of the New Testament's plan that you have completed:

___ Hearing the gospel message (Romans 10:17).

___ Believing in Jesus as the Son of God (John 8:24).

___ Determining to turn away from sin [repentance] (Acts 2:38).

___ Publicly confessing that Jesus is the Son of God (Romans 10:9).

___ Being baptized for the remission of sins (Acts 22:16).

F. Examine God's plan carefully. Study each of these key passages. Have you completed each essential part of the plan? _____

★ IMPORTANT: Lesson 5 contains no new material. It only reviews what you have already learned by showing Bible examples of people responding to God's plan of salvation. Therefore, you are fully equipped now to make your own response to the grace of God. What do you need to do to be saved? _____

IV. **Conclusion**

A. You have learned God's plan for saving you. This is not a plan of human origin, but is what the Bible clearly teaches that you need to do to be saved. Is there any way that what you have learned could be wrong? _____

B. Would you like to be baptized and be a Christian? _____

> You see then that a man is **justified** by works, and **not** by **faith only**... For as the **body** without the **spirit** is **dead**, so **faith** without **works** is **dead** also.
>
> - James 2:24, 26

Are you uncertain when you should become a Christian?

Read Appendix D to see why you should be a Christian today!

Lesson 5
Learning from the Conversions in Acts

The book of Acts has been called the book of conversions because it records so many responding to the Gospel. Let's study what those people did to be in a right relationship with God.

LESSON OBJECTIVE: Understand how to be saved by observing cases of conversion in the New Testament.

I. **Jesus told the apostles to preach the gospel**

   A. "Go therefore and make disciples of all the nations, baptizing them in the name of the Father and of the Son and of the Holy Spirit" (Matthew 28:19).

   B. The book of Acts records this teaching, and the response given to it.

II. **The first gospel sermon: Acts 2:14-38**

   A. The apostle Peter preached the first Gospel sermon to a huge crowd of Jews that had assembled in Jerusalem to celebrate the feast of Pentecost. Note the key points of the sermon:

   1. Jesus was _____ (v. 23).

   2. Jesus was _____ from the dead (v. 24).

   3. Therefore, Jesus is both _____ and _____ (v.36).

   B. Verse 37 records the response of the people: "they were _____ to the heart."

   C. Peter told the people they needed to "_____, and let every one of you be _____ in the _____ of Jesus Christ for the _____ of sins" (v. 38).

   D. How many obeyed the Gospel that day? _____ (v. 41).

III. **The Samaritans: Acts 8:12**

   A. Read Acts 8:12.

B. When Philip preached "concerning the kingdom of God, and the name of Jesus Christ" (v. 12) what did those who "believed" do? They were _____

IV. **The Ethiopian nobleman: Acts 8:27-39**

   A. Where was this man from, and what was his job?
   From: _____
   Occupation: _____ (v. 27)

   B. As he rode in his chariot he was reading a passage in the Old Testament (Isaiah 53). Did he understand what he read? _____ (v. 31)

   C. Philip "opened his _____, and beginning at this Scripture, preached _____ him" (v. 35).

   D. What was the result of "preaching Jesus to him?" The Ethiopian man wanted to be _____ (v. 36).

   E. Before he could be baptized he had to do what? _____
   _____ (v. 37)

V. **Cornelius: Acts 10:34-48**

   A. Again Peter is the one who does the preaching. Notice that his message is exactly the same:

   1. Jesus was _____ (v. 39).
   2. But, Jesus rose from the _____ (v. 40).
   3. Therefore, Jesus is "_____ by God to be _____ of the living and the _____" (v. 42).

   B. Observe that the response to the preaching of the Gospel was the same as before: "Can _____ forbid _____, that these should not be _____" (v. 47).

VI. **The Philippian jailer: Acts 16:25-34**

   A. Paul and Silas were in prison for doing right, but God opened the prison with a great sign. What was that sign? _____
   _____ (v. 26)

LESSON 5 Learning from the Conversions in Acts 33

  B. The jailer was very impressed with Paul and Silas and asked one of the greatest questions of all time: "Sirs, what must I do to be _____?" (v. 30)

  C. The jailer was told to take two specific actions. What were they?

  1. _____ (v. 31)

  2. _____ (v. 33)

VII. **The apostle Paul: Acts 22:12-16**

  A. At one time the apostle Paul was known as Saul, and he persecuted Christians ferociously.

  B. While making a trip to the city of Damascus, Jesus appeared to him and told Paul of his great mistake. As a result Saul was blind physically, but his eyes were opened to the truth.

  C. What did Annanias do first for Saul? _____
  _____ (v. 13)

  D. Saul was told to do what? _____
  _____ (v. 16)

  E. That act would do what to his sins? _____
  _____ (v. 16)

  F. Was he to delay doing this? _____
  _____ (v. 16)

  G. What does this teach us about the need to respond immediately to the Gospel? _____
  _____

VIII. **Summary**

  A. Think carefully about each case of conversion that we have read. Go back and re-read the accounts God has given us in His Word, if necessary. Can we learn from these examples what God wants us to do to be saved? _____

  B. The people we read about in Acts were saved and were pleasing to God. If we do exactly as they did, can we be saved and be pleasing to God, too? _____

- C. There are four action steps that every person who was converted in Acts took. They are:
  1. Belief in Jesus Christ.
  2. Repentance of past sins.
  3. Confession of Jesus Christ as God's Son.
  4. Baptism in water for the remission of sins.
- D. Were any of these people saved before they completed all four actions? _____
- E. Can you be saved without performing the same four actions? _____

SELF-CHECK: Think about your own soul and about your own salvation. What have you already done to follow the example of those converted in Acts? What do you still need to do? Place a "C" beside the steps you have completed, and an "R" beside actions you are now ready to complete:

_____ I believe that Jesus is the Christ.

_____ I repent of my past sins and determine to live righteously from now on.

_____ I am ready to confess Jesus as the Son of God before men.

_____ I want to be baptized to wash my sins away.

★ If you are hesitant about becoming a Christian turn to Appendix D and read the helpful material "Four Reasons You Should Become a Christian Today." Appendix D begins on page 23.

IX. Conclusion

- A. The New Testament clearly reveals one plan for the saving of people's souls.
- B. People in New Testament times were not told of many different ways to be saved, but of one way, Jesus' way.
- C. You have learned what people in the New Testament did in response to the preaching of the Gospel. You have learned the

exact steps they took to be saved. When they did these things they became Christians, nothing more and nothing less.

D. Are you ready to take those steps so that you can be a Christian too? _____

Appendix A

Does God Exist?

Can a person be certain that there really is a God? What kind of positive proof can be found for His existence? Because of the revolutionary changes that belief in God necessarily produces in one's life, these are fair questions to ask. Furthermore, Bible faith is not a blind "leap in the dark." Instead, it is the sincere trust of one who has carefully weighed the evidence and made the only reasonable decision possible. This is the faith that pleases God as found in the New Testament (Hebrews 11:6, James 2:14-26).

We need to begin by discussing the nature of proving something. Generally, when we think of proving something, we envision scientists in lab coats stirring and staring at some odd solution in a test tube. After conducting various tests upon the substance in the tube, they announce their results. But, God cannot be proven in this way. He will not be put in a test tube and poked and prodded by anyone.

This does not mean, however, that one cannot prove that God exists. It merely means that other forms of testing and evidence must be used. This should not be surprising because a great many things believed today cannot be scientifically proven. For example, no one has ever seen love. It is a concept or state of being and cannot be put into a test tube and investigated in that manner. Yet, we all believe that love exists because we have seen its effects. In other words, we can infer that the emotional state of mind called "love" exists because we have seen what people "in love" do.

When proving something we must also consider the testimony of history. No one alive today ever saw Julius Caesar. You cannot put Julius Caesar in a scientific laboratory and analyze him in any way. Yet we all believe that Julius Caesar really did live and rule the Roman world hundreds of years ago. People believe this because of the evidence of history.

As Christians, we believe that by using the same sort of methods (inferring from effects and the testimony of history), we can arrive at proof that God does indeed exist. Let us turn our attention now to three such proofs.

It is a scientific law that every effect has a cause. Nothing happens in and of itself alone; it is invariably the result of one or more causes. This law, accepted by all scientists, is called the Law of Cause and Effect. It is used continually by people every day. If the weather forecaster says a bad storm is coming (a cause), people prepare their homes, take shelter, etc. because they know what effect the storm will have. We understand that there can be no effect unless there is a cause. If the storm dissipates, there will be no damage to homes and property because there is no cause. Remember, if there is no cause, there can be no effect. And, if there is an effect, there must be a cause.

We live in the largest, most comprehensive and magnificent effect ever known to humanity: the universe. As we have seen, every effect must have a cause. Now we ask: what was the cause for this effect? What caused the universe? Some would reply, "A giant explosion, the Big Bang." But we would merely ask, "What caused that effect?" If answered, "Space dust collided together." We would again ask, "And that was caused by what?" As one can easily see, the atheist's position will eventually be reduced to confessing that there was an effect for which there was no cause. Yet, science says that every effect does have a cause. Any theory of origins that does not abide by this fundamental law of science surely cannot be considered scientific! We ask the atheist again, "Where is the cause for the effect we live in?" To summarize, the very presence of this universe (an effect) argues that there must be some cause, and we believe that cause is God.

Our second proof has to do with creation itself. Psalms 19:1 states, "The heavens declare the glory of God; And the firmament shows His handiwork." We believe that one of the best proofs of God is the surpassing grandeur of this world. There is tremendous order and careful design evident in every place that we look. The relationship between the plant and animal kingdoms is an example of this design and order. Plants consume carbon dioxide and give off oxygen. Animals consume oxygen, expelling carbon dioxide. Thus, these two kingdoms provide for each other perfectly. Could such harmony be produced accidentally? Look at the way the planets orbit our sun so perfectly. When is the last time the Earth banged into Mars on its way around? It has never happened because each planet's orbit is perfectly set into place. Does this look like a solar system that has resulted from a large, chaotic explosion? Consider the human body for a moment. Its transport, reproductive, waste removal, sensory, circulatory and respiratory systems function perfectly and are far more advanced than anything a human can devise. A child's hand is capable of more complex movement than even the most sophisticated robot. There is no computer on earth that can rival the human mind in any way. For speed, storage, retrieval, and indexing of information the brain is unsurpassed. Is all of this the result of just random luck? If one was told that a wrist watch was the product of shaking watch parts together in a box, he or she would laugh and say that someone must have designed and built that watch. Likewise, the presence of our majestic universe, planet, and even ourselves argues for a Designer and Creator: God.

Finally, we consider the evidence of history. History tells us that one named Jesus came to this earth, died, and rose to live again. This history is recorded in the books of Matthew, Mark, Luke, and John. Although many have tried to discredit the testimony that is found in those four simple volumes, it has never been done. The Gospels tell us that God came to this earth, and if God came, then certainly God exists. Remember, when He came, He was seen! In order to destroy the existence of God one must be able to demolish the integrity of the New Testament.

Please understand that stating Jesus was a good man but not God, simply will not work. Christ proved that He was God by rising from the dead (Matthew 28:6), and this resurrection is an indisputable fact. Even Jesus' enemies admitted that the tomb was empty (Matthew 28:11-15). Yes, some have suggested that the authorities removed His body. However, these authorities killed Jesus to be rid of Him and His movement. The story of Jesus' resurrection only fueled that movement further. If those who hated Christianity so much had the body of Christ, why didn't they produce it, thus destroying Christianity once and for all? This would have been the death blow the enemies of Christ so dearly wanted to inflict (see Acts 4:15-18). How foolish the apostles would have looked, proclaiming a risen Lord, when His body was put on display for all to see. Christianity would never have gotten off the ground! Others say "Well, the apostles probably took the body of Jesus." This is simply not possible because armed guards watched the tomb (Matthew 27:62-66). Furthermore, all the apostles suffered severe persecution (most were killed) for preaching Jesus Christ as the Messiah who had risen again. Would those apostles have given their lives for a lie? Hardly. The apostles did not steal the body of Christ.

Some, recognizing the power of the resurrection argument, have even attempted to deny that the New Testament is reliable history. While they have found it easy to say "The New Testament is poppycock," they have found it impossible to prove such an assertion. Appendix B discusses the reliability and believability of the Bible further. However, we do note here that this attempt to evade the force of the resurrection has failed like all of its predecessors.

Accurate history tells us that no one could have stolen Jesus' body. That body is not in the tomb. This leaves only one choice: He is risen! That says so very much, not the least of which is that Jesus is God, and therefore, God exists.

We urge you to be intellectually honest with the evidence presented here. By the laws of science, inference from what is actually seen, and the testimony of history, God has been proven to exist. God is!

Appendix B

Can the Bible Be Trusted?

Many people believe the Bible is a good book, full of interesting stories and old wisdom. But is it the work of God, capable of imparting information that will affect one's eternal destiny? Unfortunately, some people answer "No." After all, how could any book be handed down for that many centuries reliably? Is the Bible the genuine document of historical facts that it claims to be?

In this appendix we want to break these questions into two parts. First, has the Bible been accurately transmitted to us today? Second, if the Bible is in its original form, is it the work of God?

Let us begin by establishing the reliability of the documents known as the New Testament. Today, more manuscripts of the New Testament exist than any other work of ancient literature. Over 5,000 of these manuscripts are written in the original Greek, and some of these are only a few decades away from the actual original works of the New Testament writers. The number of early versions and translations of the New Testament added to the Greek manuscripts of the New Testament equals over 13,000 copies of portions of the New Testament. The director of the British Museum, Sir Frederic G. Kenyon, stated, "The interval then between the dates of original composition and the earliest extant [now in existence] evidence becomes so small as to be in fact negligible, and the last foundation for any doubt that the Scriptures have been handed down to us substantially as they were written has now been removed. Both the authenticity and the general integrity of the books of the New Testament may be regarded as finally established"[1]

The reliability of the Old Testament is equally certain. The great care that the scribes took in copying it (literally word for word) assures this. These men took unbelievable precautions when copying the Scriptures. They would actually count the middle letter of a book, and if their copy did not have the same middle letter the copy was destroyed! Numbers of similarly detailed calculations were run on every copy of the Old Testament they produced, which resulted in reproductions of the Scriptures that are incredibly accurate. Furthermore, the discovery of the Dead Sea Scrolls in

1948 has provided further evidence of the Old Testament's integrity. The Dead Sea Scrolls are copies of the Old Testament that are more than a thousand years older than any manuscripts previously in existence. Careful analysis of the Scrolls has only reinforced the belief that the Old Testament has been accurately transmitted to us today.

We might also note the enormous value the archaeologist's spade has had in confirming the Bible. The Old Testament is filled with accounts of battles, cities, empires, kings, and other verifiable points of history. The New Testament also refers to reigning rulers of the day (see Luke 3:1-2) and geographical points that can be checked and verified. If the Bible is a fraud then archaeologists would be the first to point out discrepancies as they uncover plain facts that contradict the Bible records. But instead we see that, "there can be no doubt that archaeology has confirmed the substantial history of the Old Testament tradition."[2] Nelson Glueck, the renowned Jewish archaeologist, wrote that "It may be stated categorically that no archaeological discovery has ever controverted a biblical reference."[3] Even *Time* magazine was forced to admit "Time and again, archaeological finds have validated scriptural references."[4] The Bible has been established as a genuine and accurate record of ancient history.

So, we see that the documents which compose the Bible have been carefully preserved through the ages of time. But, just because we are confident that we have an accurate transmission of the original documents does not mean the Bible was written by God. How can we be certain that the Bible is not just a good book but is actually inspired of Deity?

First, one must consider the magnificent harmony of the Bible. Though it was composed by some forty different authors, who were writing over 1,500 years, its unity and continuity defy explanation. All of these dissimilar people writing at different times and places, yet the Bible is a perfect whole, develops the same theme, and speaks effectively to people's minds and hearts for over a thousand years! No person, or group of people, could compose such a work over such time. Furthermore, the various writers never contradict one another. For certain, there have been those who have claimed to find Bible contradictions, but all of these so-called errors can easily be explained by close examination of the context, theme, and structure of the verse in question. Simply put, if one does not want to believe in the Bible, there will be plenty of opportunities to dismiss it as a myth. However, a fair-minded and honest hearing of the evidence quickly shows that no human author or authors could have written the Bible.

APPENDIX B Can the Bible Be Trusted? 43

Secondly, we note the many references to scientific principles and facts in the Bible. Although these things were completely unknown at the time of writing, they have all proven to be absolutely true. For example, Job 26:7 states that the earth is suspended on nothing, which was in direct contradiction to the teaching of the day that the world sat on a man's shoulders, or was held up by elephants, etc. How could Job have known this? Leviticus 17:11-14 teaches that life is in the blood. This principle is recognized today, but it took centuries before people stopped the horrid practice of "bleeding" the sick. The Word of God has always stated that the stars and heavenly bodies were too numerous to measure or count (see Genesis 15:5; Jeremiah 33:22), but scientists continued to attempt to number the heavens until 1932. The Bible had been right all of the time! This is just a sampling of a few facts that Bible writers could not possibly have been able to research scientifically. Yet, these writers flew directly in the face of conventional wisdom and wrote the truth anyway! How could this be possible, unless an all-wise Creator directed the writing of the Bible?

Finally, we turn our attention to the prophecies of the Bible. While anyone can make vague random guesses about the future, getting some correct while missing others, the prophets of the Bible predicted events hundreds of years into the future and never missed once! Prophecies were made against great empires such as Babylon (see Jeremiah 51:58) and Assyria (see Zephaniah 2:13) while they were in their height of power and prestige. Nonetheless, the word of God came to pass, and those mighty kingdoms were destroyed. Tyre was a powerful walled city in the days of Ezekiel. Who could have known that someday it would be utterly destroyed, literally scraped off the earth? God knew, and so said in Ezekiel 26:4-5. Several hundred years later, Alexander the Great captured Tyre and then, needing building material for a causeway, had the entire city leveled and thrown into the sea! Amazingly, the Bible even predicted the religious confusion and apostasy that exists today (see 2 Peter 3:3-4 and 2 Timothy 3:7; 4:4).

The most striking prophecies in the Bible concern the Messiah and the events of His life. Note carefully that many of these things were beyond the control of Jesus Christ. Among the specific details of the crucifixion which are accurately predicted are the piercing of His side (Zechariah 12:10), the darkness (Psalm 22:2), the vinegar (Psalm 69:21), the mocking (Psalm 22:6-8), the nakedness (Psalm 22:17), the gambling for His clothes (Psalm 22:18), the unbroken bones (Psalm 34:20), the great cry from the cross (Psalm 22:1), and the broken heart (Psalm 22:14). His resurrection was forecast in Psalm 16:10; Hosea 6:2; Psalm 30:3,9; Isaiah 53:10; Psalm 40:1-2, and other places. These kinds of specifically fulfilled prophecies indicate that the Bible could not possibly be the work of humans but must be from God.

As you examine all three of these proofs, we believe that an overwhelming weight of evidence shows the Bible is an inspired book from God. We must urge you therefore, to study and obey this book which will determine the eternal destiny of your soul.

Endnotes

1. Frederic G. Kenyon, *The Bible and Archaeology* (New York: Harper and Row, 1940) p. 288.
2. William F. Albright, *Archaeology and the Religions of Israel* (Baltimore: John Hopkins University Press, 1956) p. 176.
3. Nelson Glueck, *Rivers in the Desert; History of Neteg* (Philadelphia: Jewish Publications Society of America, 1969) p. 31.
4. John Elson, "The New Testament's Unsolved Mysteries," *Time*, December 18, 1995, p. 70.

Appendix C
Using the Bible's Chapter and Verse System

The Bible was originally written in manuscript form with no divisions in each of the individual books. The epistles in the New Testament read exactly like what they are, namely letters. The Gospels were narrated accounts of Jesus' life. In the Old Testament the history of the children of Israel was recorded no differently than secular history is today. Unfortunately, due to the vast amount of material in the Bible, it was very difficult to converse or to discuss specific portions of scripture with anyone. While nearly everyone is familiar with the story of David and Goliath, how could anyone tell another person where to find the story so that they could read it? The need for a system of cross referencing the Bible is obvious.

The system now being used was developed in the middle of the thirteenth century by Cardinal Hugo. It was refined by a man named Stephens in 1551. Although it is not perfect by any means (after all, it is the work of a man not God), it has served well for hundreds of years. All Bibles being printed today use this plan. For lack of a better term we call it "the chapter and verse system." Let us see how it works.

Each book of the Bible is divided into portions called chapters. Some chapters are very long while others are rather short. Bible chapters are much shorter than chapters found in today's novels and books. Most Bible chapters can be read by the average reader in 15-30 minutes. The Word of God contains 1,189 chapters, 929 in the Old Testament and 260 in the New Testament. Each chapter of the Bible is further divided into sections called verses. A verse is a single thought or statement in a chapter. Verses, like chapters, are numbered so that they are easy to find.

The chapter and verse system has its own notation that makes it possible for anyone to locate anything in the Bible. In this notation, the book of the Bible that is being referenced is always written first. If there is more than one book by the same name, a numeral appears to indicate whether it is the first, second, or third book of that title, i.e. 1 Thessalonians or 2 Kings. If reading aloud, one would read this as "First Thessalonians" and "Second Kings." Occasionally, Roman numerals are used (I Thessalonians or II Kings), but this does not change its meaning or how it is read aloud.

Following the name of the book will be a number that indicates the chapter that is being referenced. For example: "Psalms 23" indicates the twenty-third chapter of Psalms. Finally, behind the chapter number will be a colon (:) and then another number which indicates the specific verse under consideration. Here are some examples:

Genesis 12:1—the twelfth chapter of Genesis, verse one

2 Timothy 3:16—the third chapter of second Timothy, verse sixteen

As one can readily see, this system is easily mastered. Sometimes, the notation will include a group of verses, like this: Genesis 12:1-5. This means one should look to the first five verses of the twelfth chapter of Genesis.

In the front of most Bibles there will be an index which tells the reader the page number for every book. This greatly simplifies locating the starting point for each reference. Although finding references in the Scriptures may be somewhat of a laborious process at this time, it will not be very long until a person can remember where various books are found and can zip right over to passages with ease. If there are any further questions about how to look scriptures up in the Bible, please ask the one teaching this study to help you. Enjoy reading the Bible!

Appendix D

Four Reasons to Become a Christian Today

Many people study the Bible and conclude they need to become a Christian. However, they delay for one reason or another. The Bible urges you to obey the Gospel today—right now! Here is why:

I. **You may never get another chance.**

   A. Life is uncertain. We do not know when we will die. "For what is your life? It is a vapor that appears for a little time and then vanishes away" (James 4:14).

   B. Whether from sickness, crime, or an accident, many die everyday who did not think today was their last day on earth.

   C. What will you do if you go to meet God unprepared? What if you died tomorrow?

   D. "And as it is appointed for men to die once, but after this the judgment" (Hebrews 9:27). Get ready for judgment now!

II. **You may not want another chance.**

   A. Some fail to obey the gospel because they become fixed and rooted in wrongdoing.

   B. The longer we live outside the will of God, the easier it is for us to become tangled up in more and more sin. Those ties can become very hard to break.

   C. One has said "When you are ready to quit sin how do you know sin will be ready to quit you?" Jesus said, "Whoever commits sin is a slave of sin" (John 8:34).

   D. Becoming a Christian requires a heart that is tender enough toward God to hear the Gospel's call (see Mark 4:15, 20).

   E. What activities in your future might harden your heart so that you would never want to become a Christian? Obey now—while you still want to!

III. You are putting off the beginning of life.

A. Many delay becoming a Christian because they want to "have fun" first. By this they mean that they want to pursue the way of sin. After they have "sowed their wild oats" or "grown up some" then (so they think) they will become a Christian.

B. Sinful living does provide a momentary thrill, but it is not the way to lasting happiness.

C. "The way of the unfaithful is hard" (Proverbs 13:15).

D. Jesus is the way to abundant living and happiness: "I have come that they may have life, and that they may have it more abundantly" (John 10:10).

E. Non-Christians do not believe Christianity can be such a wonderful way to live, but they have never tried it. They are fooled by the short-lived pleasure of sin.

F. Those who trust Christ and become Christians realize quickly how superior their new life in Jesus is to the old life of sin.

G. Why wait to begin the best part of life? Start serving God now.

IV. You cannot know inner peace without acting on what you have learned.

A. You have learned what the Bible clearly teaches about sin, the church, salvation, and God. What you have studied is what the scriptures teach—not an opinion of humans.

B. You know you are lost in sin.

C. You know that without God's grace you cannot be saved.

D. You also know that to be saved you must demonstrate your faith by obeying God's plan of salvation.

E. Without obedience to God, you know you stand separated from God by your sins.

F. How can anyone have inner peace without immediately acting to resolve this terrible situation? God has done His part (grace), but now you must do your part (obey).

APPENDIX D Four Reasons to Become a Christian

G. Until you obey God, your conscience will remind you constantly that you have unfinished business with the Lord. Why live like that? Become a Christian today!

V. Conclusion

A. There are many excuses to put off obeying the gospel.
   1. "I want to wait until my family can be there."
   2. "My aunt never did this."
   3. "It is not Sunday—who will baptize me right now?"

B. Yet the Bible knows of no acceptable excuse for putting off obeying God.
   1. Whatever the problem, obstacle, or excuse, we must clear it out of the way so that we can do as the Lord instructs.
   2. This is what the New Testament shows us that people did. They heard the Gospel, understood the Gospel, and then obeyed the Gospel immediately.
   3. We should do the same!
   4. "And now why are you waiting? Arise and be baptized, and wash away your sins, calling on the name of the Lord." (Acts 22:16).

> Enter by the **narrow** gate; for **wide** is the gate and **broad** is the way that leads to **destruction**, and there are **many** who go in by it. Because **narrow** is the gate and **difficult** is the way which leads to **life**, and there are **few** who find it.
>
> - Matthew 7:13-14

www.ingramcontent.com/pod-product-compliance
Lightning Source LLC
Chambersburg PA
CBHW070452050426
42451CB00015B/3448